# Co-Parenting with a Narcissist

## *A Guidebook for Targeted Parents*

### *Lifeguide Books*

*Be the subject of your own life, not the object of someone else's*

Sharie Stines, PsyD, CATC-V
*with*
Patricia Harriman, MFA

In all things it is better to hope than to despair.
-    Johann Wolfgang von Goethe

# Contents

# Introduction

*A custody battle with a narcissist is fueled by a
desire to win at all costs. The loss of control when
the marriage ends causes the narcissist to grab
the nearest weapon – the children – in an effort to
maintain or regain control.*
– Tina Swithon

Right off the bat, I want to clarify that there really is no
such thing as co-parenting with a narcissist, because
narcissists do not collaborate or cooperate with
others—nor do they parent. They are all about
positioning, placing themselves in the "one up" position,
and keeping you in the "one down" position. Not only is
this hurtful and frustrating; it is of extreme concern for
your child's healthy development.

A better title for this book is, "Parenting in Spite of the
Narcissist," because that is your reality.

So how will you raise your children when their other
parent has a personality disorder? This guidebook was
written to help you accomplish just that. You will find
practical help and real hope for your endeavor. You will
come to see that even though it is difficult and
frustrating, you can raise your children successfully, in
spite of the impact the narcissistic parent has on your
children's lives.

This book is about empowering you to take control of
yourself and your job as a parent, regardless of whether

or not the other parent is on board. Most likely, if you have been raising children with a personality-disordered individual, you have discovered that agreement is rare and that everything tends to be controlled or manipulated by him or her. You see that your role as a parent in your children's eyes is often undermined by their other parent. That is an understatement, I am well aware.

Please know, however, that this book will help you take your power back and make wise and strategic choices with regard to how your children are raised. You will have to sift through "normal" parenting issues and those that are created by the narcissist. This will be challenging. My intention for writing this book is to help build your inner strength so that you can project this onto your children and they will learn from you how to navigate challenges in life.

One thing to continually bear in mind is that who *you are* will have a lifelong impact on your children's well-being. Never underestimate this fact. No matter how dysfunctional the other parent is, try not to get caught up in making that your primary focus; instead, focus on how you can be the "alpha" parent—that is, you can be the stronger power in your children's life—not by force, but by influence. You do not have to lay down your rights, your heart, your children's rights or hearts into the hands of a master manipulator. You can teach your children what to do and you can role-model to them how to do it.

Although it is true that your children may be strongly impacted by their narcissistic parent, who looks at relationships in terms of commodity, they will also be shaped and guided by your demonstration of how to be a healthy, strong person with a meaningful life, full of empathy and love for others. Your children are not doomed because of their other parent. It is important to keep in mind that strength is built through hardship and that your children can build their own inner strength just as you can through their difficult relationship experiences. During the course of parenting your children, keep this in mind. Always hold on to hope, create positive memories, and believe in yourself—no matter what.

# How You Can Help Your Children

*What does not kill us makes us stronger.*
                                    - Friedrich Nietzsche

Seeing your children emotionally manipulated by their narcissistic parent is a sad and complicated situation. It is difficult to know how to respond. So how can you help your children when they are being co-raised by you and this type of parent? Here are some suggestions on how to navigate this difficult situation:

- **Honesty** – Give your children the gift of honesty. Talk frankly with your children about the reality of their lives, respectfully and matter-of-factly. Do not play the game of "let's pretend everything's normal." Do not contribute to your children's sense of cognitive dissonance by colluding in the belief that the "emperor has no clothes."

- **Education** – Teach your children about emotional abuse. Try to keep it as age-appropriate as possible. This can be tricky, but you know your kids—what can they handle understanding? Keep it simple and keep it real. Teach them how to not get sucked into the drama.

- **Role Modeling** – Be a good role model. Demonstrate to your children how to stay out of the narcissist's web of destruction by maintaining your own composure and sanity. Demonstrate self-compassion and empathy. Show them how to "observe, don't absorb" when in the presence of the narcissist. Demonstrate confidence and strength.

- **Managing Anger** – Since your children already have one angry parent—even if he or she is covertly angry—make sure you don't carry grudges, that you express your own anger appropriately, and keep short accounts. Learn how to take deep breaths and walk away when you feel triggered to express your anger in a damaging way. You can learn to have self-control with your own anger.

- **Reflection** – Let your children know, "I see you." Reflect back to your children truth about their feelings. Let them know you really see their pain and their struggles. Look your children in the eyes and be with them. Connect and attune with their hearts.

- **Grieve with them** – It is heartbreaking to realize that you have a parent who only sees you as an object and who can never truly be with or see you for the valuable and precious human being you are. As the other parent, who knows only too well what this feels like, you can offer a place of comfort for your children.

- **Validation** – When people spend any length of time with a narcissist, their reality, their feelings, and their intuition is constantly invalidated. Let your children know that what they feel and experience is really happening.

- **Safety** – Your children need at least one safe parent, after all they go through emotionally having a narcissistic parent: the gas-lighting, emotional abuse, double standards, invalidation, etc. They need a parent who can offer solace, warmth, stability, and flexibility.

- **How to Love** – Since narcissists do not know how to either give or receive love, they teach their children that love is a commodity, based on performance, and must be earned. Narcissists view others as objects or resources, rather than as having intrinsic value based on the interpersonal relationship. They do not know how to care about others or offer any type of compassion that is not self-serving. As the non-narcissistic parent, you must teach your children what love is.

- **Self-Care** – Take care of yourself by relaxing, reading, maintaining close friendships, enjoying life, forgiving others and finding humor. Build your life around healthy activities and communities.

At the risk of sounding alarmist, I must warn you that narcissistic parents are damaging to children. It is advised that time spent with any narcissist be limited because it engenders confusion, dissociation, brain-washing, desensitization to abuse, emotional dysregulation, and destruction to the other person's sense of intuition. Take any steps you can to minimize the damage caused to your children by an emotionally damaging parent.

That being said, also know that there is much you can do to counterbalance the effects of a narcissistic parent on your children. This can be likened to taking your children to a bonfire. You can't change the heat of the bonfire, but you can keep your children at a safe— emotional as well as physical—distance.

## Remember: You Matter Too!

*Self-preservation is the first principle of our nature.*

– Alexander Hamilton

When living in a family with a narcissist, the entire system believes that the only person who matters is the narc. Your children (and you) have been conditioned through both blatant messages and implication, that your feelings (and you) are irrelevant.

Since this is the message your children have most likely internalized, it is important for you to unteach that message. But first, you must unteach it in your own mind.

Realize that the narcissist has taught that there is always a bad guy and someone to blame—namely you. Now that you are trying to co-parent (a misnomer, by the way) with a narcissist, you must spend much of your time reeducating and un-brainwashing your children.

One of the mantras you must incorporate in your home is, "We will not scapegoat anyone."

The overt message is that no one is going to be blamed, and the covert message you are giving is that YOU will no longer be the scapegoat in the family.

In my opinion, the best defense is a good offense. Take the direct approach and explain to your children what a scapegoat is, why it is unhealthy to create one, and how it involves blame, targeting, bullying, disrespect, and a lack of personal responsibility. Teach them to own their own behaviors and feelings without casting aspersions on to others. This is a good principle to pass on to your children, regardless of your family situation.

In that vein, one thing that you may find challenging is not blaming your narcissist for everything, which requires somewhat of a balancing act—because, after all, they are the cause of most if not all the problems in your family. You must somehow figure out how to educate your children on the problems with emotional abuse and you must also be able to call it out, while at the same time not blaming your partner or your ex.

This is hard, but not impossible, if you remember that there is a difference between explaining and blaming. Explaining things and educating is an important job of a parent; role-modeling how to scapegoat and blame others is an entirely different lesson. This is the lesson we want to avoid in ourselves and undo in our children.

The way to undo any type of conditioning in your children is to have them experience a new and different reality, one full of respect for others and empathy. Provide them with an environment where people are listened to and treated kindly. Provide your children with an atmosphere that has direct and honest communication, one without an elephant in the room.

# What if Your Children Echo Narcissistic Behavior?

*In my world there are no bad kids, just impressionable, conflicted young people wrestling with emotions and impulses.*

- Janet Lansbury

As much as we tell our children to "do as we say, not as we do," the reality is that they will mimic the behaviors surrounding them. And if one of their parents is a narcissist, exhibiting behaviors that seem to result in controlling others, a child is more likely to try that behavior out.

As the healthy parent, you can start by naming and redirecting certain behaviors, for instance scapegoating, blaming or name-calling.

Reflect to them what you see them doing, such as, "I see that you believe it is okay to call me a name." Once you reflect what you see, then explain to them how unfortunate it is for them to lose their privileges, freedoms, or ability to make their own choices for a certain amount of time.

Also, in order to teach your children that blaming or scapegoating is inappropriate, role model the change in your house. When one of your children tries to blame you for something, or treat you disrespectfully, do not engage in the argument or in a debate. Just step back, take a deep breath, and make the comment, "I see that you believe you can talk to and about me this way," going on to add, "This belief is causing you to act disrespectful to me, your parent, and it needs to stop."

Depending on the age of the child, I would go on to add, "In this house we do not scapegoat others; that is, we do not blame others for any of our problems; instead, we take responsibility."

Do not debate, argue, convince, or listen to any of your children's disrespectful words. Simply role-model to them what you will do if they choose to treat you or someone else poorly. Educate them on the concept of scapegoating, and then move on.

As best you can, remember to not take it personally. Focus on their behavior—not your feelings. If you feel yourself quickly dropping to their level, ready to hurl angry words back, take a moment to:

**Breathe.** As trite as this advice may seem, remember it's common advice because it works. Stop. Breathe. Step out of the room for a few minutes if you need to. Refocus. There. Now:

**Remember that you are the mature one.** Really, as irritating and hurtful as children can be—especially if they, too, are having to negotiate a relationship with a narcissist—they are still forming, still learning. Give them time, give them this opportunity to learn.

**Ask yourself what it is you want them to learn.** It's not just about changing behavior; it's about altering and expanding their perceptions and understanding.

Remember, you're not just raising children; you're raising future adults.

**Identify your own triggers.**  Children in particular are very good at spotting and targeting our weaknesses.  It is a kind of dare, or as the child psychologist Piaget reminded us, them asking us to confirm their boundaries.  However, when they are accusing you of not knowing how to manage money—maybe after your partner withheld his/her paycheck from the household—sometimes it hits too close to home to keep our emotions out of the fray. In the moment, you can recognize your vulnerabilities and insecurities, and after you have handled your child's behavior, take the time to journal or otherwise address your own issues.

**Remember to breathe**.

## Parental Alienation Syndrome

While this may seem like what all children do—alienate their parents—there is a particularly toxic and hurtful version of this when one parent is narcissistic. It results in the narcissistic parent manipulating the children to avoid, reject, and disdain the other parent. It is called Attachment-Based Parental Alienation Syndrome and will be covered in depth in the next few chapters.

# What is Attachment-Based "Parental Alienation Syndrome?"

*Every man is wise when attacked by a mad dog;*
*fewer when pursued by a mad woman; only the*
*wisest survive when attacked by a mad notion.*
                                    – Robertson Davies

(Note: The following is excerpted from C. Childress, *Foundations*, (2015))

In a normal attachment relationship, people are not interchangeable because each person is valuable in and of him or herself. However, this is not true for a narcissist. Narcissists have very shallow relationships in which people are interchangeable.

If a child is not connecting with a nurturing parent, but instead is calling him or her by their first name or a pejorative, then something is amiss in the attachment system.

Basically, children do not reject parents. Under relatively healthy conditions, no matter what a parent does, children do not reject them. When you find a child rejecting a parent then you are witnessing an inauthentic attachment system.

Children are motivated to bond with parents. Even in a conflictual parent-child relationship, the child is still motivated to bond with the parent. This is a typical attachment experience between a parent and child. In "parental alienation," we see detachment behavior, not attachment behavior. In parental alienation there is no grief response to the separation between the parent and child.

When a narcissistic parent experiences a great loss, such as a divorce, they do not feel normal grief like a typical person; rather, they experience a narcissistic wound to their fragile ego, which is manifested as anger and rejection of the other parent. The narcissist "splits" and makes the other parent all bad.

When "parental alienation" occurs, it is because the narcissistic parent has implied to the child that the other parent is the "bad" parent and is the one causing the child's pain. The child internalizes the narcissistic parent's anger and resentment toward the other parent and also rejects the other parent.

When the child is with the healthier parent, who is able to attach in a healthy way, painful emotions are brought up because the child needs/wants to bond, but they are conflicted because they have bought into the theory that this parent is bad, which leads to feelings of alienation and sadness.

When the child is with the narcissistic parent, there is no attachment motivation available because of the nature of narcissistic relationships, and the child does not feel bad. This is because when the child is with the non-narcissistic parent, he or she feels the natural grief response, which is painful, and when the child is with the narcissistic parent, he or she does not feel the grief response. The child interprets this incorrectly, thinking that they feel bad because the non-narcissistic parent is abusive.

Suffice it to say that the syndrome is created by the personality-disordered parent by means of covert manipulation of the child based on the disordered parent's delusional beliefs and ego defense mechanisms which are activated by the threat of abandonment by the other parent. The disordered parent's early attachment system model is in full operation and the un

healthy parent feels the threat of early attachment trauma.

## Characteristics Commonly Found in "Alienated" Parents (or other Alienated Relationships)

*Do not look for healing at the feet of those who broke you.*
— Rupi Kaur, *Milk and Honey*

If you've ever experienced the rejection of a child or other important relationship, then I'm sure you'll find the following observations compelling. Know that these insights are offered to give you a perspective from which to begin understanding and navigating the dynamic of Parental Alienation.

Being on the receiving end of a rejection can be devastating. Whether it's a boss, a parent, or a relative, the pain can be very difficult to contend with. If it's your child, you tend to feel particularly vulnerable.

Most parents, when rejected by a child, tend to think of everything they did wrong, or maybe that "one" thing they did wrong that could have caused the rift, playing over and over in their minds how they could have changed that "one" thing. Please know that it is more complicated than that, and at the same time often more about your own fears and vulnerability than anything you have done or not done.

First of all, common characteristics of people who are on the receiving end of parental alienation are:

- They are available.

- They are guileless.
- They are powerless.

Following is a discussion of each of these traits.

**Available**: Children rarely reject unavailable or abusive parents. Usually when that happens, it is not without a great amount of anguish and grieving. When a child alienates a parent, s/he does so with impudence. S/he experiences no sense of loss or regret. Instead, feels relieved. Internally, the child knows s/he could have the rejected parent back at any time. This emboldens the child and helps him/her realize that there is no great risk in rejecting the available parent.

**Guileless**: People who are guileless tend to be "innocent and without deception." Guileless individuals usually project their innocence onto others and don't see why they are being rejected, because it is not something they, themselves, would ever do to anyone. Alienated parents are usually not interested in playing dirty or fighting unfair.

The rejecting child is usually psychologically manipulated by the other parent or other important person (who is willing to fight dirty) to reject the guileless parent. It is a form of propagandizing the child and is akin to the mob effect of bullying.

**Powerless:** The rejected parent has somehow demonstrated a feeling of low power to their rejecting child. The shrugging of the shoulders and the attitude of, "what can I do?" comes to mind. This parent has insinuated to their rejecting child that the child has the power, not the parent. This usually happens in narcissistic relationships where the other parent imputes power into the child, causing the child to believe that he has more power than the rejected parent.

**The Trump Card**

This nails the coffin on the relationship. It is not a characteristic of the rejected parent, but it is an essential ingredient in the alienation process.

This involves the occurrence of a flaw, mistake, or failure on the part of the alienated parent. This failure is capitalized on by the narcissist or alienating other as evidence of the rejected parent's inadequacy. The alienated parent usually "owns" his/her failure and everyone believes it is so egregious that that parent has lost his/her value in the parent-child relationship.

Please know, however, that all is not lost. And there is no need to punish yourself further by feeling badly for your "flaws" of being nice and playing fair. What you *can* do is reclaim your power in ways that develop and cultivate well-being in you and your children.

# How to Respond to Narcissistic Parental Alienation Syndrome

*A man never sees all that his mother has been to him until it's too late to let her know that he sees it.*

- W.D. Howells

To recap, therapeutically speaking, Attachment-Based Parental Alienation Syndrome (PAS) is the unhealthy coalition between a narcissistic parent and his or her children against the targeted, non-narcissistic, non-abusive parent. The innocent or targeted parent receives hostility and rejection from his or her children in this system. The psychological health of the children is used as arsenal in the narcissist's twisted world.

The symptoms of PAS are:

- The children sit in judgment of the targeted parent's adequacy and competency as a parent.

- The narcissistic parent covertly encourages, empowers, and rewards the children for this behavior.

- The narcissistic parent feigns innocence in this process.

- The children believe they are acting independently (that is, they believe they are not being influenced by the alienating parent).

The system is created as the alienating parent rewards the children when they say hostile or angry things about the targeted parent by encouraging and displaying "understanding" for the children's negative feelings, when what should really be occurring is the children should be taught to respect the other parent. In essence, the children are gaining acceptance from the narcissistic parent as they complain about the target parent.

For instance, suppose the targeted parent tells the child to do a chore and the child resists, as is so often the case with children being told to do something they don't want to do. Now, suppose the child goes to the narcissist and complains about the "mean" other parent. The narcissist will then sympathize with the child, encouraging him or her to feel victimized by the "outrageous" expectations of the targeted parent, and will excuse the child from having to do the chore. Thus, the child is getting sucked into the web of PAS.

The targeted parent is outraged, bewildered, hurt, and betrayed. The child has been covertly empowered to disrespect the one parent who is actually trying to develop a decent human being. The narcissist sits back, effortlessly creating the destructive coalition with his or her child.

In essence, the children are "empowered" to disobey, disrespect, and disregard the non-narcissistic parent. On the surface, the children feel and believe they are benefitting and winning, but in reality they are playing a sordid part in the narcissist's perverse mind games. Not only are these mind games hurtful and discouraging, they often result in detrimental effects to the children because:

- Children's sense of value is diminished because they believe the targeted parent is unworthy of being identified with. If the children have any interests or traits similar to the rejected parent, then the children will be forced to reject those aspects of themselves as well.

- A child's character is damaged as he or she is covertly rewarded to be disrespectful, entitled, rude, judgmental, condescending, ungrateful, parentified, and hateful.

- The children develop a toxic bond to the alienating parent, as he or she manipulates them into fearing a lack of acceptance from him or her.

If you are a victim of PAS, here are some suggestions for you to try to help turn things around:

- **Be proactive**. Do not believe this problem will just go away on its own. It will most likely get worse.

- **Realize that there is not much you can do** about the alienating parent. You can only change yourself. Take a good look at your own behaviors and modify where necessary (more on that later).

- **Be a strong parent**. Do not roll over easily, no matter how angry your children may be with you.

- **Find ways to attach with your children** every day. Even if they don't want you to. Call them, text them, talk to them, touch them; do whatever you can to connect to your children.

- **Be solid.** Be direct. Be firm. Be consistent. Be stable. Even if you don't feel those things, act as if you do.

- If at all possible, **find a good therapist** who understands PAS and bring yourself and your children to see him/her.

- **Use strategies akin to those used when people leave a cult**; in essence, PAS is a form of brainwashing.

- **Take very good care of yourself.** Do things that are good for you and bring you joy.

- **Do not grovel, beg**, or allow your children to see that you are threatened by their behavior. Stand strong.

- If the narcissist encourages your children to disobey you, **hold your ground** and make sure your children do what you request, starting with "no disrespectful behavior in the home." Period.

- **Develop some catch phrases** to use with your children that you can say in moments when things are particularly difficult for you to handle.

- **Use humor.** Be enjoyable to be around.

- **Be smarter than the narcissist**.

- **Be determined**, and refuse to let the abuser destroy the relationship between you and your children.

- **Educate yourself.** Never stop reading and arming yourself with knowledge. In addition to this, educate your children.

- **Join a support group** so you can get help as you deal with this battle for your children.

Realize that you are dealing with a form of psychological manipulation of your children in which they have been brainwashed to respond toward you in hateful ways because they are being psychologically rewarded by having a pseudo-interpersonal relationship with the other parent, whom the children perceive as more powerful. Remember this as you go forward. And continue to go forward.

## What You Can Do for Yourself If You Are the Alienated Parent

*You can't pour from an empty cup. Take care of yourself first.*

- Developgoodhabits.com

If any of us want to change our environment, or our relationships, the first thing—sometimes the only thing at the moment—starts with ourselves. Here are some key activities that you can initiate to begin the process of renegotiating your relationship with your children:

- Look for local groups on alienated adults.

- Think outside the box and have a paradigm shift when raising children with another parent who is a narcissist.

- Develop friendships with people that treat you with kindness and empathy.

- Reflect to your children how you see them treating other people.

- Teach your children that you will not be a scapegoat.

- Try to get an expert mental health professional, knowledgeable about PAS, to see your children and write a letter to court.

- Try to minimize your children's time with their other parent.

- Don't listen to other people's advice unless they understand perfectly what you must contend with.

- Take care of yourself.

- Be self-affirming. Realize you are healing from the trauma of being in an abusive relationship with a mentally ill person.

- Remind yourself that you are an amazing, strong, brilliant woman or man and that you can do this.

- Be the alpha in your relationships with your children and your partner or ex.

- Don't "future trip," that is, don't predict the future and scare yourself with "horribilizing" thoughts. Just live in the current day.

- Do not let your children manipulate you with your fears of being - _____ (fill in the blank; e.g. controlling, mean, crazy, etc.)

Finally, live one day at a time. Even if you have no contact with your child today, you have no way of knowing what tomorrow may bring. None of us does. The best thing we can do is to live the best way we know how today. When you can focus on one day only, you feel less hopeless and desperate. Remind yourself, "I cannot predict the future."

## What You Can Do for Your Children If You Are the Alienated Parent

*The road may be a rough ahead, but stay the course!*

- RK3, Artist

Of course, in spite of, and in addition to, feeling hurt and rejected, your heart breaks for your children when they have alienated themselves from you. You can't help them if they won't have anything to do with you, but you need to be there as their parent the best way you can.

First of all, there are a few things NOT to do if your child or children are caught in the web of parental alienation:

**Make sure you never give your power away,** particularly to the other parent or your child. If others give you grief, never "buy in" to it or give up on yourself. Do not be weak and unstable. Try not to cry in front of your children frequently or demonstrate how powerless and weak you think you are. If you do any of these things, then your children might feel more secure around their narcissistic parent because s/he is always so confident and self-assured, while you appear to be a "wreck." Make sure you never let this happen.

**Do not act like a peer to your child.** Remind yourself that you are the parent and are the decision-maker in the relationship. It is always healthy to teach your child that his or her opinion is valuable, but in the case of parental alienation with a disrespectful child, negotiation needs to be done in such a way that your child knows who's in charge (and it's not him/her). Children feel more secure when their parents set the boundaries.

**Don't be controlling**. The goal is to get your child to choose, freely, without you controlling his decisions. This will be difficult because you don't want them to choose to be disrespectful to you. So you have to figure out how to demand respect and give him/her the freedom to choose to respect you. Remind yourself this is a psychological battle. That means, if you try to control your child then psychologically s/he will resist and polarize, going further into the trap of the alienating parent.

Instead, focus your energies and your actions on the following:

**Realize you are in a psychological battle.** Act accordingly. That is to say, before you say anything to your alienating child, think about how the child feels and will feel when you talk. For example, many parents try to convince their child to do something, making statements such as, "It will be so much fun, please come with us." If you think psychologically, what must your child be feeling after such a statement? Shall we wager to assume that s/he will feel more valuable than the parent and will act accordingly?

To wage a psychological battle with parental alienation, ask yourself some key questions. How does what I say and do affect my child? Am I reinforcing poor behavior? How can I help my child feel secure with me? Am I giving the impression that the narcissist has all the power?

**Think in terms of relationship energy.** Present yourself as the "alpha" in the relationship. That is to say, demonstrate strength and confidence at all times. Do not let your child see you sweat or know if you ever feel worried about losing him/her. Your child will play off the energy you exude. Make sure your child feels your strength and knows YOU are in charge, not him/her.

Don't worry about being perceived as cruel. Realize that being a strong parent gives your child a sense of security. As long as your child knows you are in charge s/he does not have to manipulate you through life to get his/her way. With security, your child can rest assured that everything will be okay because you are making sure of that.

**Demonstrate empathy.** Remember, you need to counteract the dysregulation of the other parent. Empathy from you must be mirrored at all times. This is not the same as being a doormat or wimp. This just means you seek to connect with confidence, you look your child in the eyes, you touch him/her with warmth; in essence, you are role-modeling what your child needs to learn and experience.

**Reflect.** Do not have a power struggle with someone hell bent on alienating you. Instead, simply reflect what you see. "I see that you are very angry with me and say that you don't want to spend time with me." Keep in mind that reflecting is mirroring. You are acting like a mirror to your child, repeat what you hear your child say.

You can also paraphrase what you hear him/her saying. When your child says, "I hate you!" "You ruined our family!" You simply say, "Wow, you are really mad right now," or, "You feel that your family is destroyed, which is really painful."

**Listen** (without personalizing.) Practice active listening. Listen more than you talk. Don't interrupt, disagree, or evaluate. Try not to spend any time in your head thinking about what you're going to say next. Simply focus on what the other person is saying.

**Wait.** Don't act like you are in a rush to get things "fixed." Act like you have all the time in the world. Remind yourself, "easy does it." Try to not make every interaction an urgent situation.

**Remind yourself that you want *voluntary agreement*.** In other words, you don't want to have to coerce your child into a relationship with you. Let your child make the decision to be in the relationship. You job is to put yourself in his/her place and imagine how s/he feels. Don't make assumptions, really give it some thought. Then you can figure out how to get your child to have the feelings of wanting to be with you.

You will win your child over by exerting your influence on him/her. This will happen after you practice empathy and active listening.

**Hold on to yourself.** Make sure you keep yourself in check. Regardless of the grief you get from the other people in your life, hold on to who you are and trust yourself. Remind yourself that you need to stand strong and be stable. Even if you don't feel like it—pretend. You can act yourself into a healthy emotional state. Remind yourself not to give your power away to any other person, including your child.

Remember that people do that which gives them a reward. Your child is a person and acts on this same principle—as everyone else. Your child is alienating you for a reason. Perhaps s/he feels that s/he will win the love of the narcissist better if s/he rejects you. Or, perhaps you seem weak and s/he doesn't respect you because you present weakness to him and in the narcissist's world, strength is of utmost value.

Children tend to gravitate toward strong, confident people. They don't feel safe around adults who don't have good boundaries and don't generate strength. Rebellious kids want adults to prove themselves to be worthy of respecting. Try to get inside your kid's head and understand what his/her payoff is from alienating you. This information will help you figure out how to win him/her over.

## How to be a Good Role Model to your Children

*Being a role model is the most powerful form of educating.*

- John Wooden

Are you a good role model for your children? Evaluate your own "defects of character," and determine how you can become a positive role model for your children. A recommendation for accomplishing this is to do a personal inventory on your own parenting to determine what you need to do to show your children how to live well.

Remember, you do not have to be a perfect parent. Remind yourself that you just need to be "good enough." Children do not benefit from having perfect parents. They just need parents to demonstrate how to navigate life. Show your children how to manage difficult relationships. Be someone strong who can help them feel secure as they experience a narcissistic person in their lives.

Evaluate the following areas of your life in order to see where you are and where you want to be. Being strong in who you are is the best position from which to go forward, for you and your children. This is a process— give it time. To begin with, ask yourself:

- What are my values? What are the principles I live by?

- What are the top three things I want my children to learn from me?

- What are my biggest weaknesses? What can I do to help myself in my weak areas?

- Am I a good listener? If not, how can I improve?

Show your children resilience. Teach them that you can overcome hard things, and as they watch, they too, learn how to overcome hardships and navigate challenges. You become the example for your children to follow. They can imprint and integrate your actions into their lives. This happens as you live out your values.

# Final Thoughts

*Nothing in life is to be feared. It is only to be understood.*

- Marie Curie
-

It is my sincere hope that you will take these perspectives and lessons to heart, be encouraged, and incorporate these strategies into your life and your interactions with your children.  Remember, even if progress feels slow, it is continually moving you and your children forward to a healthier relationship.

Below I have recapped and expounded on the principles in this book:

**Remind yourself that you are the parent.** Don't ever forget this. Also, remind your children of that same fact. Even if your partner or ex is convinced that you are not worthy of being a parent and even if s/he's managed to persuade the children into relegating you to a lowered position, refuse to cooperate. Maintain a no-nonsense attitude that you are in charge. Do this no matter what. Remember it's all in your energy. Remind yourself to generate "parent" energy, rather than "sibling" energy. (I have often seen many parents acting like one of the siblings rather than like a parent in these situations.}

**Be happy**. Your kids are not going to want to hang around with a depressed person. Even if you don't really feel happy, and even if you are downright miserable, pretend. Act as if. Just focus on things in your life that you can be grateful for and enjoy, and then try to do the things you enjoy. If possible, do them with your children. For instance, if you like to garden, do that. If you like to cook, then cook. Play music; sing; dance. Do happy things and exude happy energy. A narcissist who is full of hatred and anger will exude negative energy—most of the time. Be a contrast to this, by radiating positivity. I don't mean to be a Pollyanna, but I do mean to be realistically happy.

**Hang around with people who treat you with respect.** One thing your children need to witness is something other than what the other parent has presented to them—that you are to be disrespected and disparaged. In order to influence your children, let them see that you are a respected person. This will help them realize the only person who disrespects you is their other parent (and his/her minions).

**Display an aloof demeanor.** Do this when your children seem to be rejecting you. Don't let them feel any energy of desperation on your part. They have been trained by their other parent to capitalize on weakness. Don't give them anything to capitalize on. If you can act as if you don't need their approval, you will be that much ahead of the game. This will confuse your children because they have been conditioned to believe that they can manipulate you with your weak areas.

**Connect emotionally with your children.** I know this seems contradictory to the previous suggestion, but it isn't. Connecting emotionally is something the narcissistic parent is limited at or incapable of. In the other parent's world, your children are merely objects to be manipulated and used to generate "supply" from, and what better supply than that of hurting the other parent, by depriving him/her of the enjoyment of parenthood. You can connect emotionally to your children with attunement and resonance.

**Don't talk bad about the other parent.** You don't want to put your children in the position of having to defend the other parent. The best way to avoid that is to avoid attacking him/her. Act as if you believe it's important for your children to love and respect their other parent, even if you hate him/her yourself. If your children want to complain about their other parent, simply listen to them and validate their feelings. Use reflective listening and try to encourage them to talk about their own experiences with the other parent. Remain neutral and simply listen and provide healthy feedback.

**Educate your children.** If your children are behaving poorly toward you, each other, or anyone else, remind them that abusive behavior is unacceptable and that it is your job to teach them right from wrong. As a parent, it is important for you to equip your children for adulthood. Teach them how to be respectful, kind, non-abusive, and empathic. This includes their attitude. If your children are displaying any sort of disrespectful attitude, make sure you directly call it out and educate them on the importance of developing appropriate character. Let them know that under no circumstances are you going to overlook disrespect of any kind.

**Create an alliance with your oldest child.** This is an added recommendation, specific to families with more than one child in the family.   In that case, usually the oldest child gets manipulated away from you first, and then, with the collusion of the other parent, the other children may follow suit. The best way to prevent this from occurring is to keep the oldest child aligned with you. You do not do this by talking bad about the other parent or being narcissistic yourself; you do this by wooing. How does a person get wooed? You do this by being there and caring about him/her, by meeting your child's felt needs, by asking his/her opinion and showing empathy, concern, and genuine love for this child. This is not to say that you ignore the other children, no, not at all. This is just to say, be intentional and when you see an open door, walk through.

**Seek professional therapy, and legal counsel if necessary.** Record any evidence of parental alienation and psychological abuse and manipulation you know about that is perpetrated on your children. You may need legal help to maintain custody of your children. Find a good attorney who understands divorce from a narcissist. If your child tells you that the other parent was talking negatively about you to them or to someone else, add that to your documentation, include as much detail as you can, including dates and times.

**Refuse to need anyone's approval.** This is both hard and simple to do. Be resolute about this. Your children do not need to feel you needing their approval, period. When your kids are being brainwashed to reject you, the last thing they need to feel is that you need their approval. This will give all your power away. You need to be personally empowered to win this psychological battle. This means be mentally strong and emotionally healthy. Remind yourself that your power does not reside in any other person—only yourself.

Finally, live the moments and take the steps needed to reweave the fabric of your relationship with your children. Continue to remind yourself that you can do this.

# References

Badenoch, B. (2011). *The Brain Savvy Therapist's Handbook.* New York, NY: W. W. Norton & Company.

Ballard, Z. (2014). Stop Spinning, Start Breathing: A Codependency Workbook for Narcissistic Abuse. Zari Ballard

Bancroft, L. (2003). Why Does He Do That: Inside the Minds of Angry and Controlling Men. New York, NY: The Berkley Publishing Group

Banks, C. (n.d.) Disrespectful Child Behavior? Don't Take It Personally. Empoweringparents.com https://www.empoweringparents.com/article/disresp ectful-child-behavior-dont-take-it-personally/?utm_source=Empowering+Parents+Newsle tter&utm_campaign=78c63f83ff-Newsletter_+2018-11-06&utm_medium=email&utm_term=0_5bbf2964fe-78c63f83ff-112732713&goal=0_5bbf2964fe-78c63f83ff-112732713&mc_cid=78c63f83ff&mc_eid=98a959366d

Beatty, M. (1992). *Codependent No More.* Center City, MI: Hazelden, Org.

Childress, C. (2015). Foundations: An Attachment-Based Model of Parental Alienation. Claremont, CA: Oaksong Press.

Dahlgren, R. (2008). Time to Teach: Encouragement, Empowerment, and Excellence in Every Classroom. Hayden Lake, ID: Center for Teacher Effectiveness.

Durve, A. (2013). The Power to Break Free: Surviving Domestic Violence. Cleveland, OH: PowerPress LLC.

Lehman, J. (2015). *5 of the Hardest Things Parents Face: How to Handle the Most Challenging Parenting Issues.* Retrieved from: http://www.empoweringparents.com/the-5-hardest-things-parents-face-and-how-to-handle-them.

Simon, G. K. (2011). *Character Disturbance: The Phenomenon of Our Age.* Little Rock, AR: Parkhurst Brothers, Inc.

Simon, G.K. (2010). In Sheep's Clothing: Understanding and Dealing with Manipulative People. Little Rock, AR: Parkhurst Brothers, Inc.

Steinbeck, J.T. (2017). *The 5 steps to begin reversing alienation.* Retrieved from: http://www.brainwashingchildren.com/the-5-steps-to-begin-reversing-alienation/

Van der Hart, O., Nijenhuis, E.R.S., Steele, K. (2006*). The Haunted Self: Structural Dissociation and the Treatment of Chronic Traumatization.* New York, NY: W. W. Norton & Company.

Made in the USA
Coppell, TX
13 July 2021